Reclaiming life, one poetic breath at a time

I AM MY OWN HOME

KERRY PARSONS, PMHNP.

I Am My Own Home

© [2025] by Kerry Parsons, PMHNP.

All rights reserved.

No part of this book may be reproduced, stored in a retrieval system, or transmitted in any form or by any means—electronic, mechanical, photocopying, recording, or otherwise—without prior written permission from the author, except for brief quotations used in reviews or articles.

Published by Pine Tree Press

www.pinetreepress.com

For permissions or inquiries, please contact:

www.intertwined.love

Printed in the United States of America

This book is a work of creative nonfiction. While drawn from the author's lived experience, names and identifying details have been changed to protect the privacy of individuals. The reflections within are offered for inspiration and connection, not as medical or mental health advice. Please seek professional support if you are in crisis or in need of care.

To everyone carrying the weight of becoming:

You are not broken. You are coming home to yourself.

DEDICATION

For those who loved me when I could not love myself —

the ones who stayed long enough for me to learn how.

For every heart still softening into its own rhythm,

and every soul still finding home.

ACKNOWLEDGEMENT

To the hugs that held me steady,

the hearts that reminded me why I began,

and the quiet moments that whispered me back to truth.

To my family and closest friends — there are no words to express my gratitude for standing

beside me through seasons of uncertainty, growth, and grace.

Your belief in me was a compass when I felt lost.

To my clients, who show me daily the courage it takes to return home to oneself —

Your journeys inspired every page.

To my mentors and creative collaborators,

who remind me that we are here for the obstacles

and that softness is strength.

And to the Earth — my first teacher, constant mirror, and steady anchor.

You reminded me that home was never something to find,

only something to remember.

This book is an offering born from each of you.

AUTHOR'S NOTE

Darling Child,
I don't know what brought you here.
Heartache. Burnout. Longing.
Maybe it was the quiet ache of not feeling quite like yourself anymore.
Whatever it was/is, it is a privilege to have you here.

This book was born from my own return to self, through pain, tenderness, and practice.

It is not a how-to guide.

It's a collection of truths I learned the hard way.
Of breathwork between breakdowns,
Of rituals born from needing to survive.
Of grace, after so much gripping.

I wrote it for the part of us that's tired of performing.
For the part, that's curious to know if there's another way.
For the part that knows, deep down, you were never broken, just buried.
I am honored to be a companion as you walk home to yourself.

With gratitude, love, and deep reverence,
Kerry Parsons, PMHNP.

The Sacred Return

INTRODUCTION

This book is not about becoming someone new.
It's about remembering who you've always been.
It's about honoring what is true in your body,
even when the world tells you to override it.
It's about learning to stay with yourself.

Especially when it's hard.

It's about reclaiming the parts of you that were abandoned
in the name of survival, belonging, or being "good."

Over the years, I've had the privilege to sit with people in the rawest moments of
their lives, through trauma, transition, collapse, and evolution.
And I've walked through those landscapes in my own body, too.
What I found wasn't a fix.
It was a rhythm.
A slow, steady return to self.
That's what this book is:
A rhythm.
A return.
A conversation between soul and body.
It moves in poetic fragments,
stories, truths, rituals, reflections, and breath.
You don't need to read it in order.
I invite you to follow your intuition. Let your body lead.
Begin wherever you hear a gentle yes.
Each chapter offers a soft structure:
A lived truth, a moment of insight,
a journal invitation, and a breath to return to.
Not as a prescription, but as permission.
Permission to be messy.
To go slow.
To begin again.

You'll find themes of nervous system healing, boundary repair, body wisdom, grief, self-belonging, and the slow bloom of becoming.
You'll hear stories of collapse and resilience, shame and sacred Nos, love lost and confidence found…not because I have it all figured out, but because I've lived enough to know that
presence is more powerful than perfection.
I hope these pages help you slow down. I hope they offer you language for what you already know deep inside. I hope they help you return—not to a version of yourself that you miss, but to the wholeness that's always been waiting underneath.

Welcome home.

The Tender Art of Staying

It didn't happen all at once.
I was sitting in my car, music blasting, hands gripping the steering wheel as if
bracing for an oncoming semi-truck.
There was a fluttering behind my ribs…
a restless ache, an old ghost of urgency.

The ache of wanting to run.
To disappear before something hurt me first.

Knowing better didn't silence the pull.

Knowing better didn't erase the map my body still carried:
the one that said,

when it hurts, leave.

But this time, I stayed.

Dopamine is the fuel of pursuit.
It whispers, just one more—
one more scroll,
one more task,
one more attempt to feel enough.

In a world where gratification sits at our fingertips,
understanding the biological pull of dopamine offers liberation.

Not every pull deserves obedience.
Luckily, awareness now helps me use it to my advantage.

For a long time, I mistook perseverance for virtue.

But sometimes, quitting is the holiest thing you can do for yourself.

Slowly, I began to see where I had fawned into autopilot,

agreeing,

staying,

adapting.

Not because it was true,

but because it was safer.

I learned to listen to my body:
the fluttering chest, the hollow stomach, the wired exhaustion.

Letting myself into these raw places was the bravest thing I've done.

It was not weakness.
It was reclamation.
It was the tender art of staying.

REFLECTIONS AND INVITATIONS
The Tender Art of Staying

Staying doesn't always mean holding on.
Sometimes it means softening into the moment without abandoning yourself.

The tender art of staying is not about endurance; it is about discernment.
It is the willingness to pause when your body whispers "leave,"
and to gently ask:
Is this fear...or is this just familiar?

Staying means choosing presence over the reflex to flee; not by force, but by curiosity. It is not about staying in pain or harmful situations, it is about staying with yourself in the truth of the moment.

This matters because so many of us learned to survive by running, fawning, or numbing. But real safety is not found in abandoning ourselves; it is found in reclaiming our breath, our body, and our voice.

Practice by noticing your sensations, by asking gentle questions, and by allowing yourself to release what no longer aligns. Sometimes staying looks like breathing through discomfort; sometimes it looks like quitting what was never meant for you. Both are holy.
The act of staying, especially when staying is new, is a profound and sacred gesture of self-loyalty.

REFLECTIONS AND INVITATIONS
The Tender Art of Staying

Take a breath. Let the following invitations guide your reflection:

- ❁ What are the moments or situations in my life where my body says, "run?"
- ❁ What sensations accompany this urge? Where do I feel them?
- ❁ When have I mistaken endurance for alignment?
- ❁ What did it cost me to stay silent, agreeable, or invisible in those moments?
- ❁ What does "quitting as a sacred act" mean to me?
- ❁ Is there a part of my life right now asking to be released or reimagined?
- ❁ What does it look like to stay with myself, even in discomfort?
- ❁ What does it feel like in my body when I choose presence instead of pattern?
- ❁ Who or what has helped me feel safe enough to stay?
- ❁ How can I begin to offer that same safety to myself?

The Courage to Be Seen

There was a time when visibility felt dangerous.
When standing out felt like the same thing as standing alone.

I learned to tuck away the parts of myself that felt too loud, too tender.

I carried my softness like contraband,
smuggled away in the quiet corners of my heart.

I learned the art of disappearing.
To take up less space.

To quiet the tremor in my voice.

To soften my edges so I wouldn't cut anyone,
least of all myself.

But something happens when you hide your tenderness for too long.

It begins to harden.

It calcifies in the spaces where it should have flowed freely.

And in its place, I found restlessness.

The ache of a self, unspoken.

Learning to stay with myself was the beginning.

Learning to carry that tenderness into the world,
that has been the deeper work.

When I stopped hiding from my tenderness I noticed it everywhere.

In the tremble of laughter,
In the crack of a voice,
In the soft, unspoken moments between strangers.

It became a language I could finally understand.
I could recognize it in others because I had finally welcomed it back into myself.

Tenderness became a bridge.

A way to connect.

A sacred form of strength.

The parts of me that I once believed were liabilities became the very threads that wove me back into the world.

But carrying my tenderness into the world is not without risk.

I had to learn a balance between openness and self-preservation.

To allow myself to be seen
but not devoured.

To hold my softness
but not surrender it.

Boundaries became vital.

Not walls, but thresholds.
Not barriers, but gateways.

An invitation for only the ones who could meet me there, gently, carefully, reverently.

Discernment became sacred.

The ability to know the difference between those who seek to witness and those who seek to consume.

To carry my tenderness into the world required boundaries, yes, but it also required belonging.

First, to myself.

To know that my softness does not need permission.

That it does not need to be palatable to be worthy.

The courage to be seen is the courage to first belong to myself.

To gather my tenderness,

to cradle it in my hands,

and to offer it…

not to be taken,

But to be met.

REFLECTIONS AND INVITATIONS
The Courage to Be Seen

Being seen isn't about performance.
It's about presence.
It's about allowing your realness—not your readiness—to step into the light.
Tenderness is not weakness.
It is the living pulse beneath your protections,
the quiet courage it takes to stay open in a world that taught you to close.
To be seen is to carry your softness into the world, even when you've been conditioned to hide it.

Because denying tenderness only hardens it into restlessness, the ache of an unspoken self. When welcomed back, tenderness flows again, weaving you into connection with yourself and others. By offering your presence as an invitation, not as a spectacle. By holding boundaries like thresholds, spaces of safety where your truth can be met, not consumed.
When you choose to carry your softness into the light,
you aren't just expressing yourself,
you're offering a quiet invitation:

"Meet me here, not as a spectacle, but as a mirror."

To be seen is to risk.
To be seen is to belong to yourself first,
unfiltered, unpolished, utterly whole.

REFLECTIONS AND INVITATIONS
The Courage to Be Seen

Let this reflection be a return to that belonging.

- ❀ What parts of myself have I hidden in order to feel safe?
- ❀ What did I fear might happen if those parts were fully seen?
- ❀ What does tenderness feel like in my body right now?
- ❀ If I imagine cradling it in my hands, what does it need from me?
- ❀ Where in my life am I still softening my edges to keep others comfortable?
- ❀ What might it feel like to show up with my full texture, without diminishing my truth?
- ❀ What is the difference, for me, between being witnessed and being consumed?
- ❀ Who in my life has offered safe, sacred witnessing?
- ❀ What are my boundaries protecting me for...not just from?
- ❀ Can I reimagine my boundaries as invitations, thresholds for intimacy rather than isolation?
- ❀ If I stopped asking my softness to be palatable, what would it say? What would it do?

Somatic Prompt:
Meeting Yourself in the Mirror

Find a quiet space where you won't be interrupted.
Stand or sit in front of a mirror, somewhere you can see your face, your eyes, your expression.

Let your breath arrive slowly, gently.
Place one hand on your heart, and one on your belly.
Feel the rise and fall.
Feel the warmth of your own presence.
Now, softly meet your own gaze.
Not to critique, not to fix,
but simply to witness.
Let your eyes say:

"I see you. I'm here."

Notice what arises:
tightness, emotion, resistance, tenderness, longing.

Let it all belong.

If tears come, let them come.
If a smile arrives, let it arrive.

Breathe.

You are practicing the art of sacred witnessing,
with yourself as the honored guest.

Let this moment be enough.

The Slow Bloom of Becoming

True belonging isn't given.

It is reclaimed.

It comes in small, ordinary moments:
choosing rest,
honoring "no,"
celebrating the quiet revolutions of self-honoring.

Sometimes, belonging to myself meant loneliness.

It meant boredom.

But it also meant standing on solid ground for the first time.

It is better to stand alone in truth,
than to be adored in abandonment.

Belonging to myself was not the end.

It was the root.

Becoming is the bloom.

It is the slow, sacred act of offering my full self to life without waiting for permission.

Becoming did not come as a lightning strike.

It came in ordinary choices.
Quiet refusals.
Invisible shifts.

The world worships sudden change.
But real growth is slow, stubborn, and unseen.

You are not behind.

You are blooming at the speed of trust.

Stillness is not failure.

Silence is not stagnation.

The in-between is where the roots grow strongest.

It is preparation,
not punishment.

Healing has its own sacred calendar.

You are not late.

You are not broken.

You are blooming right on time.

You are not here to be perfected.

You are a breathing, unfolding, evolving life.

You are holy in your becoming.

You don't need to rush, fix, or prove a thing.

What's blooming inside of you is sacred.

And it is more than enough.

REFLECTIONS AND INVITATIONS
Belonging and Becoming

Take a deep breath.
Close your eyes if that feels safe.
With each inhale, return to your root.
With each exhale, soften into your becoming.
There is no clock you must race.
There is no prize for hurrying.

Becoming is not about speed;
it is about trust.

It is about reclaiming yourself in the quiet, ordinary moments,
choosing rest, honoring "no," listening to your own timing.
Belonging does not arrive as a gift from the world.
It blossoms from within.
Every self-honoring choice, no matter how small,
is evidence that you are already here.
Already whole. Already home.
When urgency whispers that you must rush, prove, or shrink…pause.

Remember: stillness is not failure.
Silence is not stagnation.
This in-between is sacred ground.
You are not waiting for life.
You are living it, now.
You are already becoming.

REFLECTIONS AND INVITATIONS
Belonging and Becoming

- ❀ Where am I still dimming my light in order to keep connection, rather than honoring truth?
- ❀ What parts of my life ask me to be smaller than I truly am?
- ❀ Where have I already begun to practice belonging to myself?
- ❀ What does it feel like in my body—physically, emotionally, energetically—when I choose myself?
- ❀ Where might I be ready to carry my tenderness into connection, even if it feels vulnerable?
- ❀ What roots within me have quietly grown stronger over this past season or year?
- ❀ What might it feel like to trust my own timing, even if others don't understand it?
- ❀ What permission can I offer myself now, as I continue to bloom in my own rhythm?

Somatic Prompt:

Place a hand over your heart and another over your belly.

Feel the rhythm of your breath beneath your palms.

Imagine this as the rhythm of your becoming.

What does your body know about trust, about readiness, about timing?

How does it react when you ask these questions?

What sensations do you feel?

Let it speak.

A Short Letter from My Heart to Yours

My friend,
If you ever wonder whether it's working—this slow,
tenderly tending to yourself,
know this:

It is.

You are blooming in ways the world does not yet know how to see.

Stay with yourself.

Trust your roots.

You are sacred exactly as you are.

With deep reverence for your becoming,

Kerry

Living at the Pace of My Own Life

There is nothing easy about choosing to live differently than you were programmed to.

To pause. To notice.

To choose a conscious response over a habitual reaction.

It takes energy. Intention. Self-trust.
It is not a mindset shift.

It is a full-body retraining.

It is a practice.

Some days, it feels like I'm rewiring my nervous system with a single breath, over and over again.

And it only works if I care for myself like someone I believe in.
I had to start giving myself the same compassion I so freely offered others.

Why was I kind to everyone but myself?

Why could I make room for the humanness of others,
but criticize every place I hadn't arrived yet?

There were thoughts I had to name.

Patterns I had to examine.

Responses I had to admit were not coming from grace,
but from wounds.

And still…I work at it.

Not because I'm broken.

But because I am finally choosing not to abandon myself.

I ask myself…

What grounds me?
What makes me feel connected?
Why do I still choose things that disconnect me sometimes?

Because healing is a spiral.

Because self-loyalty is a muscle.

Because I still need practice.

And that's okay.

I've learned to ask a harder question when I'm trying to be helpful:

Does helping this person hurt me?

Sometimes the answer is hard to admit.

Sometimes it means walking away from someone I still love,
someone who could never love me in a way that let me thrive.
I wanted him to prove everyone wrong. I still do, sometimes.

But I've finally learned how to care for myself,

And now,

I trust my gut.

Living at the pace of my own life means listening to the part of me that rises with the sun and wants to dance in the evening light.

It means tending to my body with castor oil, turmeric, long baths, music, and laughter.

It means living in rhythm with what feels like home:
animals, water, friends, mountains, creativity, sweat, stillness.

It means knowing what makes me feel alive and choosing it, over and over.

It means giving myself permission to spend my energy where it nourishes me, and permission to reclaim it when it doesn't.

This life I'm building doesn't need to be understood by everyone.

It just needs to be lived by me.

Fully.

Honestly.

At the pace that honors both my spirit and my nervous system.

This is my tempo.

This is my rhythm.

Rooted.
Regulated.
Real.

This is my life.

REFLECTIONS AND INVITATIONS
Finding Your Own Rhythm

Choosing to live at your own pace is never a straight path; it is a spiral, a rhythm you return to again and again. Some days it feels effortless, other days it feels like you are actually building a house by hand, in the heat, with no water. Both are part of the practice.

Instead of rushing to fix or critique, try listening. Listening to your body. To the subtle shifts in your breath. To the quiet wisdom that rises when you pause long enough to hear it. This is where your true rhythm lives. Not in the expectations of others, but in the pulse of your own becoming.

REFLECTIONS AND INVITATIONS

Finding Your Own Rhythm

Let these questions guide you back to yourself, not as a checklist to complete, but as gentle invitations to re-root:

- ❀ What grounds me? How can I bring more of this into my daily life?
- ❀ Where am I softer with others than I am with myself? What would it feel like to extend that same tenderness inward?
- ❀ What patterns, habits, or relationships pull me out of my rhythm? What shifts might happen if I began to release them, even slowly?
- ❀ Does helping here cost me more than I can afford? Am I offering from love, or from self-abandonment?
- ❀ What is my natural tempo? How could I honor it—even in one small way this week?
- ❀ What would it mean to care for myself like someone I truly believe in? What choices would reflect that belief?
- ❀ If I trusted my intuition fully, right now, what would I choose?

You don't need to rush toward the answers. Let them land in their own time. The practice is not in knowing, it is in listening, honoring, and moving at the pace of your own becoming.

Rewiring the Response

Belonging to myself meant living at the rhythm of my own life.

It meant honoring the spaces where I moved too quickly,
where my nervous system still flinched at shadows.

Slowing down gave me room to notice,

to feel the surge of old patterns,

rise like a tide and breathe through it

instead of being swept away.

There is something sacred in pausing before the reaction.

A breath,

a space,

a whisper that says:

"You can do this differently, this time."

Sometimes I wish people knew just how much energy it takes to not react the way I used to.

To feel my chest tighten, my ears grow hot, my stomach twist in knots,

and still,

to not flee.

Not fawn.

Not collapse into the familiar shape of survival.

It's like standing in a river as the current tries to drag me under—
my only job is to plant my feet,
hold my breath,
and remember that I am stronger than I once was.

That moment…

where I stay with myself instead of abandoning myself,

is where everything begins to change.

But it's not easy.

It never has been.

Rewiring a response is not a single decision.

It's a practice of real-time awareness of feeling the surge and not letting it take the wheel.

It's hearing the whispers…
"You are not safe."
"You are too much."
"You have to fix yourself before they leave."
…and choosing,

not to believe them.

Now, I check in first.
I breathe.
I place a hand over my heart or feel the earth beneath my feet.

I ask myself gently:

What's happening in my body right now?

What story am I telling myself about this moment?

Is this fear, or is this truth?

Some days, I get it right.
I breathe through it.
I soften my jaw,
unclench my fists,
speak from my heart,
let tears flow.

Other times, I spiral.

I shut down.

I forget everything I've learned.

But even then, even when I go back to an old pattern, there's a new awareness watching.

A part of me is saying:
That didn't feel good.
But I think I know why I did it.
And I can choose differently next time.

That is rewiring, too.

Healing doesn't mean you never get activated.

It means you learn to recognize the patterns,

to move more slowly within them,

to return to yourself faster afterward.

It means your compassion shows up before your shame does.

It means you forgive the part of you that panicked, and offer yourself a different way forward.

No…it's not always graceful.

Many times, especially at the beginning,
it is messy,

raw,

inconsistent.

But I am learning that there is grace in the mess.

That healing is not a straight line,

It is a spiral,

looping back to old lessons with a softer heart and a deeper breath.

Sometimes I can feel how hard my system is working to not shut down, and all I can do is rest afterward.

Because this work takes something real.

It takes sleep.

It takes food that nourishes the brain.

It takes breath and sunshine and a body that's been moved.

It takes space.

It takes specific frequencies.

It takes time.

Rewiring a response is not just about willpower.

It's about capacity.

And I have to build mine every day.

So do you, darling.

I don't owe anyone perfection.

But I owe myself presence.

I owe myself the dignity of checking in
before I hand the moment over to a younger,
frightened version of me who didn't know better.

When I pause long enough to breathe,

I can feel her there,

the younger me who had to defend,

who had to shut down to survive.

And instead of letting her take the wheel,

I put my hand on my heart and tell her,

"I'm here now. I've got this."

I am not trying to be a better version of who I used to be.

I am trying to be a more honest, more attuned version of who I am now.

And that is sacred work.

REFLECTIONS AND INVITATIONS
Honoring Your Capacity

Rewiring isn't just about reacting differently.

It's about relating differently, to yourself, to your body, to the stories that rise up in moments of stress.

It's about creating enough space inside to pause, to notice, and to choose again.

This isn't willpower.

This is capacity.

And capacity is something you build with your daily choices.

It takes:

- Rest that you treat as sacred, not optional.
- Food that nourishes your brain and soothes your system.
- Breath that expands what's possible and releases what no longer serves.
- Sunlight that reminds you warmth still finds you.
- Movement that brings you back into rhythm with your aliveness.
- Stillness that offers integration, without rush or pressure.

You don't owe anyone perfection.
But you do owe yourself presence.

REFLECTIONS AND INVITATIONS
Honoring Your Capacity

Presence to check in before you hand the moment over to an old pattern.

Presence to ask:
Is this reaction coming from safety or survival?
What would help me feel just 5% more anchored right now?
You are not here to become a shinier version of who you used to be.
You are learning how to be an attuned, rooted version of who you already are.

That is brave.
That is sacred.
That is enough.

- What does capacity mean to me at this point in my life?
- When I feel overwhelmed, what helps me stay with myself instead of abandoning myself?
- What messages does my body send when I'm triggered? Where do I feel them?
- What's one old pattern I'm learning to interrupt? What helps me soften or shift it?
- When do I feel most disconnected from my breath or body? What could I offer myself in those moments instead?
- What might it look like to respond from presence rather than from pattern?
- Who or what helps me feel safe, steady, and seen—without needing to perform or please?
- What does it mean to treat myself like someone I trust?
- What truth am I ready to speak to myself with love, not judgment?

Somatic Prompt

Place one hand over your heart, and the other on your belly.

Feel your breath rise and fall beneath your palms.

Without needing to change anything, simply ask yourself:
What am I feeling right now?

What do I need right now?

Let the answers come slowly. Even if they're silent, even if they're unclear, your willingness to ask is the beginning of rewiring.

Energy Is Currency

There came a moment in my healing where I realized:

My energy is sacred.

And I was spending it like I didn't care what it cost me.

I gave it to people who didn't listen.

To expectations I never agreed to.

To guilt that wasn't mine.

To spirals I didn't want to be in.

To conversations that left me wrung out and resentful.

And then I'd wonder why I felt disconnected, depleted, dysregulated.

The truth is:

Every interaction, every obligation, every mental loop costs us something. And just like with money, if I don't track where it goes,

I end up in deficit.

I had to start treating my energy like it mattered.

Because it does.

Some days, this means pulling back before I feel depleted.

Not waiting until I'm undone to realize I've overextended.

Asking: Does this give me life or take it away?

It means pausing before I jump in to help…and asking myself honestly:

Does helping this person cost me something I can't afford to give today?

Because I've learned:

Self-abandonment is the most expensive thing I own.

And I've paid for it far too many times to keep pretending I can afford it.

My energy goes where I want it to now:

To the sun rising over the mountains.

To the salt of the ocean.

To slow mornings and long walks and late-night laughter.

To tending the space between who I am and who I'm becoming.

To people who see me clearly…
not as a fixer, a therapist, a container,
but as a human.

A soul.

A being with needs of her own.

My energy is my currency.

And now, I spend it like it's worth something.

Because it is.

Because I am.

I am not a resource to be mined.

I am a force to be honored.

And so are you.

REFLECTIONS AND INVITATIONS

Honoring Your Energy as Sacred Currency

Take a slow breath.
Feel your feet anchored to the ground.
Place a hand over your heart or rest it on your belly.
Notice: what does energy feel like in your body right now?
Not the story of what you should be doing,
but the truth of what you are carrying.
Imagine your energy as light: warm, luminous, alive.
It is not infinite.
It is not owed.

It is yours.

To protect.
To honor.
To spend wisely.

Let these invitations meet you where you are, not to fix, but to illuminate.

REFLECTIONS AND INVITATIONS
Honoring Your Energy as Sacred Currency

- ❋ Where am I overspending?
- ❋ Which obligations, roles, or dynamics leave me depleted, no matter how much I give?
- ❋ Where am I spending out of guilt or habit instead of desire?
- ❋ What would shift if I released those unspoken "shoulds?"
- ❋ Am I investing in relationships, practices, or places that return energy to me?
- ❋ How can I redirect my reserves toward what replenishes me?
- ❋ What hidden "fees" are draining me?
- ❋ Which mental loops, self-criticisms, or internal negotiations cost me more than I realize?
- ❋ If my energy is currency, what are my worthy investments?
- ❋ Which rituals, relationships, or environments yield the greatest sense of connection and aliveness?
- ❋ What boundaries act as my savings account?
- ❋ How might I create energetic reserves by saying no—or by saying yes more selectively?
- ❋ What permission slip do I need to write myself today?
- ❋ How would it feel to stop apologizing for honoring my limits?

Somatic Prompt:

After answering these reflections, lie down or sit comfortably.

Close your eyes and visualize calling all your scattered energy back to you.

From every place you've overextended, from every conversation you left feeling unseen.

Let it return like soft light gathering at your center.

You do not need to earn rest.

You are allowed to keep something for yourself.

Remember:
Your energy is sacred.
Let how you spend it reflect how deeply you value your own life.

Rituals of Return

When I spiral, I don't shame myself anymore.
I return.
I come back with rhythm.

With ritual.

With sensory truth.

Not punishment.
Not restriction.
Not urgency.

Just a gentle,
steady coming home.

There was a time when I believed I had to fix everything in one single, breathless moment.

I'd sprint toward resolution, reaching for urgency instead of understanding.

I would tighten my grip, bracing against the storm of my own discomfort.

But that isn't healing.
That is survival disguised as growth.

Real healing is softer.

It is the tender act of returning;
not once,
but again and again.

Returning to my breath.

To my body.

To the quiet corners of my heart that whisper,

You are allowed to begin again.

Over time, I learned what brings me back.

Not harshness.
Not rigid perfection.
But rhythm.

Ritual.

Sensory truth that anchors me when the world feels unsteady.

The sun, rising and setting,
reminds me that I can start over and soften.
I watch it pour itself across the sky each morning,
whispering to the earth that there is still time.
That I have right now.

Water anchors me.
It cleanses.
It opens.
It reminds me of flow,
of softness that wears away even the hardest stones.

Earth calls me home.
I bury my hands in soil and remember that I am still here.
Still sacred.
Still becoming.

I fill my life with the things that remind me I am connected to all of this.

Apples with honey.
Rosemary and oregano oil.
Lavender.

Medicines from the earth that say: you are worth tending to.

The flickering of a candle.
Wind moving through grass.
Birds singing.
Stretching.
Hammocks.
The beat of a drum.
Dancing.
Watering my plants.
A dog wagging his tail at me.
Sunbathing.
Talking to the people who actually see me…

not the polished mask, but the messy, magical, human truth.

None of this is luxury.

It's survival.

It's how I stay.

These rituals aren't perfectionism.

They are permission.

Permission to begin again.
Permission to slow down.
Permission to be a whole human who needs care.

There is no straight path back to myself.
There are only practices of remembering.

Of coming home, over and over.

I used to think returning to myself meant I had failed.
That I should have been strong enough to hold on the first time.

But healing is cyclical.

It is looping back to old patterns with a more open heart and steadier breath.

It is the willingness to come back to the softness of my own soul,
again and again,

without shame.

These rituals are my anchors.
They tether me when I begin to drift.

They are not luxuries; they are survival.

They are sacred.

Because every time I return to myself,

I reclaim a piece of me that I once left behind.

REFLECTIONS AND INVITATIONS
Rituals of Return

When the world feels too loud, when the spiral begins, returning to yourself is not a failure, it is a sacred act of grace.
Not through urgency. Not through force.
But through rhythm, through ritual, through the gentle remembering of what steadies you.

Rituals are not indulgences.
They are how we anchor.

They are how we stay.

REFLECTIONS AND INVITATIONS
Rituals of Return

Let these questions be a soft place to land as you explore your own rituals of return:

- What sensory experiences bring me back to myself?
- When have I felt most present in my body? What sights, sounds, textures, smells, or flavors help me feel grounded?
- What simple rituals help me feel connected and steady?
- Are there practices, like lighting a candle, drinking tea, moving my body, tending to plants, or watching the sky, that return me to center?
- Where in my life can I make more space for these rituals?
- What small shifts in my environment or routine would invite more presence?
- What does a gentle return look like for me?
- When I feel lost, overwhelmed, or spiraling, what would it feel like to come back softly instead of harshly?
- What does it mean to give myself permission to begin again?
- If I believed every breath was a new beginning, how would I treat myself differently?

You are not too much.
You are not too late.
You are already in motion, spiraling not away from yourself, but toward deeper truth.

When you're ready, you may wish to try this short meditation to embody your own ritual of return:

A Ritual of Return

Take a breath.
Let it move all the way down into your belly.
Let your shoulders drop.
Let your jaw soften.
Exhale slowly, as if your body is sighing in relief.

There is no rush.
There is no performance.
There is only this breath.

Place a hand over your heart or anchor your feet into the earth.
Feel what's touching the ground beneath you.
Notice the way the air moves in and out of your nose.
Let your awareness spiral inward.
Let this be a gentle homecoming.
You don't have to fix anything right now.
You don't have to prove or perfect.
You are simply remembering that you belong to yourself.

Ask gently:
What does my body need in this moment?
What would bring me just a little more comfort, warmth, or ease?
What sensation reminds me that I am here?

Breathe again.
You are allowed to begin again, as many times as it takes.
Returning is not a weakness.
It is the rhythm of healing.
It is the root of becoming.

Let your next breath be an offering.
A whisper to yourself:
I am still here.
I am still scared.
I am home.

The Confidence That Comes After

After I cleared what was no longer true, what stayed was clarity.

And in that clarity, I found a kind of confidence I didn't know I'd been looking for.

Not the loud kind.

Not the kind that needs to convince or explain.

But the quiet, rooted kind.

The kind that speaks without rushing.

That moves without asking permission.

That stands, not because it needs to be seen,
but because it finally knows it belongs.

This confidence wasn't born from certainty.

It came from grief.

From truth-telling.

From the slow, steady release of what was never really mine to carry.

I had to let go of the roles I played so well.

The caretaker.
The peacekeeper.
The one who stayed quiet so others could stay comfortable.

There was a time I let people's opinions live rent-free in my head.
I made space for them, rearranged my thoughts to accommodate them,
hosted their doubts and projections like honored guests.

I treated my inner world like a home with unlocked doors,
anyone could walk in, critique the decor,
take pieces of me with them when they left.

I was telling myself it was generosity.

It wasn't.

It was self-abandonment.

True confidence, I've learned, is a kind of emptying.

A clearing out.

Not a gathering of louder voices, gold stars, or endless validation,
but a sacred quieting of the noise that never belonged to me.

And in that quiet, I began to hear myself again.
Not the echoes.
Not the shoulds.

Just me…clear, calm, and unshakably present.

I stopped handing out the key to my peace.

I stopped letting everyone's needs come before my nervous system.

I stopped letting other people's opinions
echo louder than my own knowing.

Now, when someone projects, I don't rearrange my furniture.

I don't open the door just because they knock.

I know who I am when the room is silent.

I know what it costs to betray that knowing.

I no longer choose that cost.

Everyone is entitled to their opinion.
But they are not entitled to shape my reality.
They do not get to redecorate the sanctuary I've rebuilt inside myself.

This is the confidence that comes after.

After the grieving.
After the clearing.
After the boundaries have been drawn in salt and ash and gold.

It is earned.

It is sacred.

And it does not ask to be understood.

It just is.

REFLECTIONS AND INVITATIONS
Returning to True Alignment

This chapter was never about becoming louder.
It was about becoming clearer.
About peeling back the layers that never truly belonged to you.
About noticing the subtle ways you gave away your peace to be liked,
silenced your truth to preserve connection,
confused people-pleasing with love,
or accommodation with safety.
Confidence, the real kind...arrives in the quiet aftermath.
After the unraveling.
After the roles have been released.
After the noise has settled.
It comes when you begin to hear the sound of your own voice again.
This reflection is not about building something new.
It's about noticing what has stayed.
What has remained steady when everything else has been cleared away.
This is your chance to explore what is asking to be honored,
what feels undeniably true,
what roots you when doubt or old patterns try to move back in.
Take your time.
Let the answers rise like breath,
like soft shoots through soil,
unhurried, unforced, entirely your own.

REFLECTIONS AND INVITATIONS
Returning to True Alignment

- What have I recently let go of that no longer felt true?
- How did it feel in my body to release it? What sensations told me I was ready?
- What roles have I played to feel accepted, understood, or safe?
- Which ones am I ready to retire with compassion and gratitude?
- What does quiet, rooted confidence mean to me?
- How is it different from the kind I've performed or chased in the past?
- Whose voices still echo in my mind when I doubt myself?
- Which ones am I ready to turn down, or release entirely?
- Where have I allowed others to "redecorate" my sense of self?
- What am I reclaiming now as mine alone?
- What is the sound of my own inner knowing?
- How does it speak, whisper, warmth, sensation, and how can I practice trusting it?
- What boundaries protect my peace?
- Are there any I feel ready to clarify or strengthen with grace?
- In what areas of my life am I becoming more honest—with myself, and with others?
- Where does this honesty create more alignment and freedom?
- What truths have emerged now that I've cleared away the noise?
- How do I feel them rooting into my life?

If confidence is an emptying,
what am I still holding onto that no longer serves me?
What might I discover in the space that remains?

Somatic Prompt:

Centering the Self

Place one hand over your heart and the other over your belly.

Breathe deeply into this space.

Feel your body rise with breath and soften with release.

Ask yourself gently:

What am I holding that isn't mine?

What am I ready to release so I can return to myself, fully?

Stay here for a few breaths.
Let the answers come or not come.

The pause is the practice.

Affirmation

I am no longer shaped by who others needed me to be.

I am rooted in who I truly am.

My voice matters.

My peace is sacred.

My clarity is enough.

Decisive but Distracted

I've never been indecisive.

If anything, I've always been the one people look to when things fall apart.
I can scan a situation and act.
I can delegate, fix, manage, move.
That kind of decisiveness has served me.

But it has also cost me.
For a long time, I mistook movement for momentum.

I thought being good at navigating chaos meant I was headed in the right direction.

I confused urgency with purpose.
Action with alignment.
Survival with success.
I assumed I was becoming someone
because I was doing something,

But doing is not the same as becoming.

And certainty is not the same as clarity.

I threw myself into projects, people, plans…
Thinking if I just stayed busy, it would all eventually make sense.
But effort doesn't always equal meaning.

And not all motion is forward.

I am decisive.

But I was also distracted.

Distracted by things that looked like purpose
but were actually performance.

By validation loops and emotional labor.

By applause in rooms by people that didn't see me.

By the sense that my worth lived in what I could offer,
not who I am.

I spent my energy in places that praised my generosity
but never returned it.

I could make decisions.
But I wasn't making choices.

Eventually, I paused...

long enough to interrupt the autopilot.

Long enough to ask some questions that actually matter to me:

Whose vision am I moving toward?
Is this desire mine, or did I inherit it?
Do I actually want this, or am I just good at it?

Those questions changed everything.

I started noticing where I was giving my energy.

How much of it went to keeping up the performance.

How often I moved with urgency, not intention.

How I kept running, chasing acceptance, chasing proof, chasing "enough."

I began to clear what wasn't true.

And in that clearing, I heard something else:

My own rhythm.

My own voice.

The steady confidence that comes after.

Not from the rush of action, but the spaciousness of stillness.
Not the kind of confidence that needs to convince anyone.
But the kind that doesn't seek permission because it's not looking for approval.

The kind that doesn't explain itself.
That knows belonging doesn't require performance.

I realized:
I can be good at something and still not want it.

I can execute flawlessly and still not belong to it.

I can contribute without choosing to continue.

So I stopped spending energy where it wasn't met.

I stopped setting myself on fire to keep others warm.

I stopped saying yes just because I could.

I started leading myself back to my vision.

I started saying no,
not because I was too busy,
but because I am too important to abandon.

Confidence, it turns out, is not volume.

It's ownership.

It's belonging to yourself so fully
that no one's departure leaves you empty.

No one's criticism shakes your knowing.

It's not rushing to explain.

It's not contorting to fit.

It's not exhausting yourself to be palatable.

It's standing steady in your own becoming,
knowing that what is true does not need defending.

That's what alignment feels like.

It feels like gentleness.

It feels like clarity.

It feels like not needing to be understood.

REFLECTIONS AND INVITATIONS
Decisive but Distracted

For so long, decisiveness may have been your survival skill.
A way to move forward.
To manage chaos.
To be the one who acts when everything is falling apart.

But there's a difference between movement and momentum.
Between leading, and leaving yourself behind.
Between doing, and becoming.

It's easy to confuse performance with purpose.
To mistake urgency for alignment.
To believe that action means progress, simply because you're moving.

But there is power in the pause.
In stopping long enough to listen.
To check in.

To ask the questions that matter.

REFLECTIONS AND INVITATIONS
Decisive but Distracted

As you reflect, hold these questions not as demands for answers, but as invitations to return to what is true for you now:

- ❀ Whose vision am I moving toward?
- ❀ Is the path I'm on truly mine, or shaped by someone else's expectations?
- ❀ Is this desire mine, or did I inherit it?
- ❀ What parts of my ambition feel rooted in my truth, and which are borrowed stories?
- ❀ Am I chasing validation instead of fulfillment?
- ❀ Where have I confused applause with alignment?
- ❀ Is this actually what I want, or just what I'm good at?
- ❀ What might shift if I pursued what nourishes me, not just what I perform well?
- ❀ Where am I mistaking action for alignment?
- ❀ What would it feel like to slow down and move with intention, not urgency?
- ❀ How can I begin to interrupt the autopilot?
- ❀ What rituals or moments of stillness help me reconnect to my deeper knowing?

Ritual of Reclamation:
Clearing and Keeping

Find a quiet space.
Take a breath.
Let your nervous system settle.
Light a candle if that feels supportive.
With pen and paper, draw two columns.
Label one: "Clear."
Label the other: "Keep."

In the Clear column,
write down what no longer belongs to you:

Expectations you've outgrown
Narratives that dim your light
Patterns of over giving or urgency
Desires you inherited but never chose

In the Keep column,
name what brings you back to yourself:

The people who see you clearly
The dreams that still stir in your belly
The rhythms that feel like home
The quiet confidence that lives beneath the noise

When you're ready, read the lists aloud.
Let each word settle.
Notice what shifts in your body as you speak the truth of what you're clearing...
and what you're choosing to keep.
This is reclamation.
Not a performance, not a plan,
but a return to your vision.

A Soft Pause Before We Continue…

Before you move into the next chapter, I offer you this note as a moment of breath,
a reminder, a recalibration. Let it settle where it needs to.

From My Heart to Yours…
May you remember:
Your life is not something to rush through.
It is something to live in.
Moment by moment.
Breath by breath.
May you give yourself permission to slow down,
to soften,
to choose rest over proving,
and presence over perfection.
May your nervous system become your compass,
guiding you not by urgency, but by truth.
And may you wake up each day knowing:
You are allowed to live your life in a way that makes sense to your body,
your heart,
and your spirit.
You do not need to ask for permission.

You are the permission.

Living Consciously in a Chaotic World

The world is loud.

It pulls in every direction toward comparison, overstimulation, distraction, urgency.
There is a constant hum beneath it all,
a tugging at my attention,

a whisper that I am not enough unless I am everything.

I've had to learn how to live with it,
without letting it live inside me.

To watch the waves of urgency crash against my peace without letting them sweep me away.

I can get overwhelmed easily.
By arbitrary rules,
litter,
too many people talking at once.

There are days I want to crawl out of my skin and into a quiet place where no one wants anything from me.

But I've learned not to disappear.

I've learned to stay conscious.

Not by numbing or fighting everything at once,
but by getting fiercely intentional with where I place my attention.

The world will always offer chaos,

but I can still choose how I respond.

And that choice is where my power lives.

The world will always offer chaos,
but I can still choose how I respond.
And that choice is where my power lives.

I breathe.
I unplug.
I say no to invitations that cost me clarity.

I used to think I had to hold everything,
to absorb it all like it was my responsibility.
Every headline.
Every opinion.
Every person's urgency.
But I am learning that I am not the container for anyone else's chaos.
I do not have to carry the world's noise in my bones.
I do not have to hold it all just because I am capable.
I can choose to let it pass by.
I can watch it swirl and thrash,
knowing I am not required to join its rhythm.

I ask:
"Does this bring me closer to the life I want to live?"
"Is this helping me connect to the only life I am conscious of living, or just
distracting me from myself?"

A mentor once told me:

"You can only change the world from the seat you sit in."

So I take my seat every day.

I sit in mine with presence.

I place my feet on the ground,
feel the earth beneath me,
and remember that my power lives in my awareness,
in my breath,

in my ability to choose.

It is tempting to try and control every seat around me,
to reach across the table and rearrange the pieces of someone else's life.

But I have learned that the most powerful thing I can do is sit fully in my own.

To know what belongs to me,
and what does not.

I used to think consciousness meant hyper-vigilance.
I thought it meant staying on guard,
anticipating every blow,
managing the chaos before it could swallow me.

But I am learning that true consciousness is not control.

It is presence.

It is the art of choosing where my energy goes and knowing that I am allowed to be selective.

I look at the clouds.
I let a cup of tea warm my hands.
I say no without explaining.
I step away without guilt.

The world is loud.

But I do not have to absorb its chaos.

I do not have to carry its weight just because I hear it.

I can still choose what I let in.

I can still choose what I give away.

I am learning to live consciously,
not as a form of resistance,
but as a form of self-respect.

I am learning to sit in my own seat and watch the world move without rushing to join its frantic pace.

To move with intention,

to respond instead of react,

to protect my peace like it is sacred,

because it is.

REFLECTIONS AND INVITATIONS
Living Consciously in a Chaotic World

Living consciously in the midst of chaos isn't about silencing the world.
It's about choosing what you let in.
It's about remembering that presence is power.
That your awareness is a sacred gatekeeper.
That you are allowed to protect your peace without apology.

Conscious living doesn't mean tuning everything out.
It means tuning into yourself first.
It means sitting in the seat of your own life with clarity, discernment, and care.
It means feeling your own breath, grounding your own body, and remembering that what you allow in shapes how you live.

REFLECTIONS AND INVITATIONS
Living Consciously in a Chaotic World

Gentle prompts for reflection:

❀ What noise am I letting in that I could turn down? What distractions or pressures pull me away from the life I want to live?
❀ Where am I saying "yes" out of obligation instead of alignment? What would shift if I allowed myself to say "no" with grace and self-respect?
❀ Does this bring me closer to the life I want to live? What happens when I pause before reacting and choose from a place of presence?
❀ Am I living from the seat I sit in—or trying to manage seats that aren't mine? How can I reclaim the power of my own attention and stop reaching outward for control?
❀ What would it look like to meet chaos with calm instead of urgency? What rituals or practices support my grounded response?
❀ How can I create intentional space for stillness and reflection?
❀ Where in my life could I gently lower the volume and deepen my awareness?

Living consciously is not about resisting the chaos.
It's about honoring your own rhythm within it.

Ritual of Conscious Choice:
Turning Down the Noise

Find a quiet space. Close your eyes.
Let your breath slow. Feel your feet on the floor, the steadiness of your breath, the beat of your own heart.
You are here. You are home.
With a pen and paper, draw two columns:

Noise to Turn Down

List the external pressures, internal loops, and energy drains that pull you away from yourself.

Be specific. This is not about shame, it's about clarity.

Peace to Turn Up

Now, list the people, practices, and places that help you return to stillness, to presence, to your own rhythm.

What nourishes your nervous system?
What reminds you that you are safe and whole?

When you're ready, read the lists aloud or silently to yourself.
Close your eyes and imagine your inner dial.
Turn the volume down on the chaos.
Turn the volume up on the peace.
Let the noise soften.
Let your breath deepen.
Let yourself come home to the quiet knowing within you.

This is how you live consciously in a chaotic world:
Not by escaping it, but by choosing how you meet it.
Rooted.
Present.
Alive.

The Kind of Love I Give (And Deserve)

I have always known how to love people.
When you're hurting,
I'll sit with you—
not to fix you,
but to remind you that you're not alone.

I have always known how to hold space for joy and sorrow,
for the heavy and the light,
for the soft places that often go untouched.

I want depth.

I want connection that feels like truth, not performance.

I want to walk with people through the long stretches of their becoming,
to sit in the silence of what is unspoken and still feel seen.

For a long time,
I thought love meant being that for everyone without asking for much in return.

I poured myself out like I was an endless resource.

I lit myself up for others,
set myself on fire to keep the room warm,
and called it generosity.

But something shifted.

A slow, soft unraveling of my own self-abandonment.

I began to wonder what it would feel like to be held the way I hold others.

To be asked how I work,

how I feel,

how I move through the world.

I started to realize I don't just want to give love that way.

I want to be loved that way.

Not in pieces.
Not in performance.
Not for how helpful I am.

But for the wholeness of who I am.

I want love that doesn't rush past my hesitation.
Love that meets me where I am,
even if that place is tender,
even if that place is raw.

I want someone to ask me what I need,

not just when I'm breaking,

but when I'm blooming.

I want to be seen,
not just when I'm strong,
but when I'm tired,
too.

But here's the hard part:
before I could ask anyone else for that kind of love,
I had to learn to offer it to myself first.
I had to learn to hold space for my own heartache,
to sit in my own silence,
to ask myself:

What do you need right now?
What would feel like love to you in this moment?

I had to stop waiting for someone else to show up with the answers.

I had to stop waiting to be rescued from my own tenderness.

I had to stop setting myself aside, thinking someone else would come along and gather me up.

I began to give what I used to hope someone else would bring.
Compassion.
Observation.
Understanding that did not demand performance or perfection.

I started asking myself the questions I had always longed for someone else to ask:

How do you feel today?
What's heavy right now?
What's lighting you up?

And in that practice,
I learned to stay with myself instead of abandoning myself.

To give the kind of love I have always known how to offer,
but never knew how to keep.

No one is coming to save me.

But I am no longer leaving myself behind.

I used to think love was about offering more of myself,
pouring out, showing up, being available.

But now I understand that love is also about keeping parts of myself.

Holding onto what is sacred and not handing it out to every passerby who promises
they'll hold it with care.

I no longer hand out pieces of me to anyone who reaches for them.

I no longer light myself on fire for warmth that isn't mutual.

I no longer perform my softness just to be seen.

I love with my whole heart.

And now I know I deserve to be loved with the same.

I am learning to ask for it.

I am learning to receive it.

I am learning to recognize when I am being given crumbs and how to step back
instead of reaching for more.

I used to think love was something I earned.

But now I understand it is something I am worthy of,
simply because I am here,
simply because I am breathing.

REFLECTIONS AND INVITATIONS
The Kind of Love I Give (And Deserve)

Loving deeply has always been our nature. Sitting with others in their sorrow, celebrating their joy, holding space without rushing to fix—these are sacred ways of being.

But love is not meant to be a one-way current. It is not meant to flow outward while you are left untended.
To truly live in the fullness of love, you must also turn that tenderness inward.

To ask, to listen, to nurture your own spirit the way you've longed for others to do.
It is not selfishness; it is self-honoring.

REFLECTIONS AND INVITATIONS
The Kind of Love I Give (And Deserve)

Here are a few questions to hold as you consider the kind of love you give... and the kind you deserve:

- Where do I give love more freely than I allow myself to receive?
- Do I offer myself the same compassion I offer others?
- How do I want to be loved, not just in concept, but in the small, tangible ways that make me feel seen and safe?
- Am I accepting crumbs when I desire the feast of wholeness?
- What would it feel like to love myself the way I've longed to be loved?
- Where can I practice asking for what I need, and what would it feel like to trust I am worthy of that ask?

Love is not only what you give away. It is also what you allow to come back to you.

Ritual of Self-Offering:
Love as an Act of Return

Find a quiet space. Light a candle if that feels right. With a journal, take a deep breath, and gently ask yourself:

What kind of love have I been giving away freely that I need to offer to myself?

Where have I been waiting for someone else to show up with the love I've longed for?

What would it look like to stop waiting?

Write these down as offerings.
Imagine gathering those pieces back to yourself.
See them returning, whole, unbroken, and yours.
Whisper to yourself:

"I am worthy of the love I desire."

Let it be a prayer, a declaration, a beginning/continuation of your becoming.

I Am My Own Home

There was no single moment when I became whole again.
No grand epiphany that wrapped everything up neatly.

Just one honest breath after another.

One brave decision.
One sacred no.
One deeper yes.

Again and again and again.

This journey hasn't been about becoming someone new.

It's been about remembering who I've always been.

It's been about unearthing the parts of me that were buried under years of adaptation, hidden beneath the clever disguises of survival.

I used to think coming home to myself meant a grand return,
a breakthrough moment where I would finally arrive.

But now I know: coming home is quieter than that.
It is the gentle unfolding.
The soft exhale.
The willingness to stay when I want to run.

To listen when I want to distract.
To hold when I want to harden.

Coming home is a practice of presence.

It means learning to live in alignment with what is true.
Not what is perfect,

but what is real.

It means honoring my realness,
my rhythms,
my boundaries,
even when they disrupt the expectations that were never mine to carry.

It's recognizing the difference between who I am
and who I was taught to be.
I've stopped waiting.

to be chosen.

to be saved.

to feel ready.

to be understood.

I used to think I needed permission.
I used to wait for someone to tell me it was okay to take up space,
to ask for what I need,
to live my life the way I imagined it.

But I've stopped waiting for permission because I realized,

I am my own permission.

I am my own invitation.

I am my own beginning.

I am my own home.

And I am not leaving.

The walls are built from boundaries.
The roof is made of reclaimed truth.
The floors are softened with self-compassion,

and the windows are open wide,
letting in only what nourishes me.

It took time to understand that home was not a place I had to find.

It was a place I had to build.

Brick by brick,
choice by choice,
I built it with everything I used to give away for free.

My energy.
My love.
My truth.

Now I belong to myself.

I live here.

I tend to this space.

I protect it from what is not meant for me.

When I get lost, I know where to come back to.

Not to someone else.
Not to some idea of perfection.

But to myself.

To this sacred ground I have built with my own two hands.

I Am My Own Home.

REFLECTIONS AND INVITATIONS
I Am My Own Home

Healing is not a single moment of triumph.
It is a sacred return, again and again.
One honest breath,
one brave decision,
one small act of self-loyalty.

It isn't about becoming someone new.
It's about remembering who you've always been beneath the noise.

Coming home to yourself means honoring your truth.

Not perfection, but presence.
Not performance, but permission.

It's no longer about waiting to be chosen.
It's about choosing yourself, fully, unapologetically,
right here,
right now.

REFLECTIONS AND INVITATIONS
I Am My Own Home

- ❄ Where have I been waiting to feel ready?
- ❄ What would shift if I began as I am, right now?
- ❄ How do I return to myself when I feel scattered?
- ❄ Which rituals or spaces anchor me back home?
- ❄ What does deep loyalty to my own life look like?
- ❄ Where have I been abandoning myself, and where am I ready to stay?
- ❄ Am I still waiting for permission, or willing to grant it to myself?
- ❄ What small, everyday acts affirm my belonging?
- ❄ What would it feel like to honor what's real instead of what's ideal?
- ❄ How can I release perfection and choose presence?
- ❄ How can I witness my own becoming without rushing?
- ❄ What helps me slow down enough to see myself clearly?

Ritual: Returning to Myself

This ritual is a doorway back to your own heart whenever the world feels too loud or you begin to drift.
Find a quiet space.
Light a candle, or hold something grounding in your hands.
Close your eyes and breathe deeply.
Now, imagine yourself walking through the front door of your own heart.
It is familiar.
Safe.
Yours.
Rest here. And ask yourself:
What parts of me have I reclaimed through this journey?
How do I know when I am truly with myself, body, mind, and soul?
Where am I still learning to stay, even in discomfort?
What truths am I now willing to speak, even if they change everything?
What kind of love do I want to give and receive, and how will I honor that today?
When you are ready, write your responses as declarations; not as wishes, but as truths you are claiming.
Speak them aloud.
Let them become your compass.
Let them be your return.

Meditation: Arriving Home
Find stillness.
Let the noise settle.
Be here, just as you are.
Place your hands over your heart.
Feel the rhythm.
The soft, steady reminder that you are alive.
That you are already here.
Take a slow, deep breath in,
down into your belly.
Let it expand, making space for all that you've gathered.
All that you've remembered.
Exhale softly,
like a prayer.
Like a promise.
There is no rush.
There is no race.
Only this breath.
Only this becoming.
You are home.
Notice the spaces within you that feel softer now,
the ones that used to brace and grip.
Feel how they open like flowers in morning sun.
Feel the ease you've earned.
You are not behind.

You are not broken.

You are exactly where you're meant to be.
Breathe in and whisper:
"I am enough."
Breathe out and whisper:
"I am my own home."
Let that truth settle in your bones.
Let it carry you forward.

A Love Letter from My Heart to Yours

Dear Visionary,
Thank you for being here.
Fully.
Bravely.
Imperfectly here.
You didn't have to take this journey.
You could have stayed on autopilot.
Held your breath.
Kept your heart guarded.
Told yourself, "This is just how I am," and turned the page.
But you didn't.
You stayed.
You softened.
You told the truth.
You touched the raw and holy places within you,
and you decided you were worth knowing.
Worth loving.
Worth coming home to.
And that changes everything.
I don't know where your path will lead from here.
I don't know what mountains you'll climb,
what heartbreaks you'll outgrow,
what miracles will unfold.
But I do know this:
The you who walks forward from these pages
knows how to return.
You know how to breathe through resistance.
How to rest when the world shouts for urgency.
How to say yes with integrity.
How to say no without apology.
How to hold your own hand when no one else understands.
You are not lost.
You are not broken.
You are not behind.
You are already enough.
Already whole.
Already worthy of the life that calls to you.

So keep listening.
Keep tending.
Keep choosing yourself, not out of ego, but reverence.
Not because you are incomplete,
but because you are sacred.
And sacred things deserve to be cherished.
Let this be your permission slip:
To take up space.
To rest without guilt.
To live softly, messily, audaciously.

To be seen.

To begin again, and again, and again.
Thank you for walking this far with me.
For letting me walk beside you.
For holding the questions.
For honoring the pauses.

For daring to come back to yourself, even when it was hard.
I hope you leave these pages not with all the answers,
but with a deeper, more loving relationship to your own questions.
I hope you wander with grace.
I hope you bloom without urgency.
I hope you let your tenderness lead.
I hope you return home to yourself...again and again and again.

You are not alone.
You never were.

With all my heart,
Kerry

Bio of Author

Kerry Parsons, PMHNP, is a psychiatric nurse practitioner, writer, and integration therapist devoted to helping others rediscover their innate capacity for healing and belonging. She believes that true wellness begins in relationship—with ourselves, with others, and with the natural world that mirrors our cycles of growth and rest.

Through her practice, Intertwined, Kerry bridges modern psychiatry with ancient wisdom, blending evidence-based medicine, depth psychology, and somatic integration to create spaces of safety and remembrance. Her trauma-aware approach invites clients to meet themselves with compassion, curiosity, and reverence for the body's intelligence.

In both her clinical and creative work, Kerry explores what it means to live in rhythm with one's truth. Her writing offers gentle guidance toward self-loyalty, nervous system regulation, and the art of staying present through change.

When she isn't writing or meeting with clients, Kerry can be found walking with her dogs, tending to her plants, and listening for the quiet lessons of the Earth—the teacher that continues to remind her that healing is not a destination, but a return.

www.ingramcontent.com/pod-product-compliance
Lightning Source LLC
Chambersburg PA
CBHW040847170426
43201CB00005BB/49